SHW

Lexile:

LSU ☐ yes
SJB ☐ yes
BL: 5.5
Pts: 1.0

A BLUE BANNER
BIOGRAPHY

Orlando Bloom

Tamra Orr

Mitchell Lane
PUBLISHERS

P.O. Box 196
Hockessin, Delaware 19707
Visit us on the web: www.mitchelllane.com
Comments? email us: mitchelllane@mitchelllane.com

Mitchell Lane PUBLISHERS

Copyright © 2007 by Mitchell Lane Publishers. All rights reserved. No part of this book may be reproduced without written permission from the publisher. Printed and bound in the United States of America.

Printing	1	2	3	4	5	6	7	8	9

Blue Banner Biographies

Alicia Keys	Allen Iverson	Alan Jackson
Ashanti	Ashlee Simpson	Ashton Kutcher
Avril Lavigne	Bernie Mac	Beyoncé
Bow Wow	Britney Spears	Christina Aguilera
Christopher Paul Curtis	Clay Aiken	Condoleezza Rice
Daniel Radcliffe	Derek Jeter	Eminem
Eve	50 Cent	Gwen Stefani
Ice Cube	Jamie Foxx	Ja Rule
Jay-Z	Jennifer Lopez	J. K. Rowling
Jodie Foster	Justin Berfield	Kate Hudson
Kelly Clarkson	Kenny Chesney	Lance Armstrong
Lindsay Lohan	Mariah Carey	Mario
Mary-Kate and Ashley Olsen	Melissa Gilbert	Michael Jackson
Miguel Tejada	Missy Elliott	Nelly
Orlando Bloom	Paris Hilton	P. Diddy
Peyton Manning	Queen Latifah	Rita Williams-Garcia
Ritchie Valens	Ron Howard	Rudy Giuliani
Sally Field	Selena	Shirley Temple
Tim McGraw	Usher	

Library of Congress Cataloging-in-Publication Data
Orr, Tamra.
   Orlando Bloom / by Tamra Orr.
      p. cm. — (Blue banner biographies)
   Includes bibliographical references and index.
   ISBN 1-58415-515-9 (library bound : alk. paper)
   1. Bloom, Orlando, 1977—Juvenile literature. 2. Motion picture actors and actresses—Great Britain—Biography—Juvenile literature. I. Title. II. Series: Blue banner biography.
PN2598.B6394O77 2006
791.4302'8092—dc22
[B]
                                                 2006014809

ISBN-10: 1-58415-515-9   ISBN-13: 9781584155157

ABOUT THE AUTHOR: Tamra Orr is a full-time writer and author living in the Pacific Northwest. She has written more than 50 educational books for children and families, including *The Dawn of Aviation: The Story of the Wright Brothers* and *Ice Cube* for Mitchell Lane Publishers. She is a regular writer for more than 50 national magazines and a dozen standardized testing companies. Orr is mother to four and life partner to Joseph.

PHOTO CREDITS: Cover—Scott Gries/Getty Images; p. 4—Avik Gilboa/WireImage; p. 7—The OB Files; p. 9—Dave Hogan/Getty Images; p. 11—Chad Rachman/AP Photo; p. 15—Dean Treml/Getty Images; p. 17—ES/Globe Photos; p. 22—Gareth Davies/Getty Images; p. 24 (top)—Globe Photos; p. 24 (bottom)—Alpha/Globe Photos; p. 27—Pascal Le Segretain/Getty Images.

PUBLISHER'S NOTE: The following story has been thoroughly researched, and to the best of our knowledge represents a true story. While every possible effort has been made to ensure accuracy, the publisher will not assume liability for damages caused by inaccuracies in the data, and makes no warranty on the accuracy of the information contained herein. This story has not been authorized or endorsed by Orlando Bloom.

CONTENTS

Orlando Bloom shows off the smile he is known for at a press conference for the film **Elizabethtown.**

One Small Jump

*I*t looked simple enough. It was one small jump — nothing to it.

In fall 1998, Orlando Bloom, 21, had decided to spend a beautiful Sunday afternoon with his friends in their apartment. Lunch was almost ready and it smelled delicious. Everyone was eager to start eating. Someone suggested that since this apartment had a roof terrace and it was a lovely day, why not eat outside?

The plan had one glitch. The door leading to the terrace was stuck. Rain had warped it. It would not budge, no matter how much Bloom and his friends pushed, pulled, and tugged. Bloom looked at the window and smiled. If he could just crawl out the window and jump over to the landing, he might be able to open the door from the outside.

Carefully, he slid out the window. He gave the drainpipe on the wall a shake. It seemed strong. Holding on to it for support, he jumped. Unfortunately, the drainpipe was in much worse condition than he had thought. Inside it had rusted so thoroughly that the shaking had loosened it from the wall. As Bloom jumped, the pipe gave way.

It was a moment he would remember for the rest of his life. In seconds, he fell three floors, landing on his back. He drifted in and out of consciousness as help arrived. It took a combination of emergency medical technicians and a crane to reach him. A brace was put around his neck. He was placed on a spine board and strapped down so that he would not move. He did not want to. He was in too much pain.

The next few days were a blur for Bloom. At the hospital, X-rays showed the worst. He had crushed one vertebra—one of the small bones in his spine—and fractured three more. He had also broken several ribs. Surgeons were called in. They warned Bloom and his family that the young man might never be able to walk again. They suspected he might live the rest of his life in a wheelchair or, at the very least, be bedridden for months.

> **"The doctors said I wouldn't walk at all," recalls Bloom. "I chose not to believe them. I thought, that's not me, that's somebody else."**

"The doctors said I wouldn't walk at all," recalls Bloom. "I chose not to believe them. I thought, that's not me, that's somebody else."

Four days after the accident, Bloom had surgery. The doctors attached two bolts and six metal plates to his spine. Friends and family held their breath. Would he be able to walk again? It was a tough time. "I experienced all these weird moments where I was exploring really dark corners

Bloom learned early that determination is a huge part of success in life.

of my mind," says Bloom. "I was lying there on my back, unable to do anything. You don't know how you're going to be under those circumstances."

To the amazement of everyone, Bloom was on crutches within days of his injury. He had a lot of physical therapy sessions to learn how to walk again. After only 12 days in the hospital, he walked out on his own. He would wear a neck brace for months and take pain medication even longer, but he was on his feet and ready to take on the world again.

His perspective had changed a bit, however. "I was very, very lucky," he admits, "and it sort of kind of changed my whole approach to life." The boy who was sure he was invincible was now a man who knew better.

From the Beginning

*B*reaking his back was just one incident in a long line of injuries for Bloom. He was an accident-prone child from the beginning.

Orlando Jonathan Blanchard Bloom was born January 13, 1977, in Kent, England, to Harry and Sonia Copeland Bloom. His sister, Samantha, was two years old.

Harry Bloom had been born in South Africa. He worked as a lawyer, and he had written a book speaking out against the mistreatment of blacks in his country. The government did not like what he had to say. He spent three months in jail, and his book was banned throughout Africa. In 1963, he moved to England and became a professor of law at the University of Kent. Sonia Bloom shared her husband's passions about racial equality, or treating people from every race equally. She helped longtime family friend Colin Stone start a school called Concorde International for foreign students who needed to learn English.

Family remains very important to Bloom. He is accompanied by his mother, Sonia (far left); his grandmother (left); his sister, Samantha (right); and Colin Stone.

The Blooms had two reasons for choosing Orlando for their son's name. First, he was named in honor of Orlando Gibbons, a 17th-century composer whom Sonia and Harry respected. Second, it was a name that Harry could easily remember. With so many college students to keep track of, he tended to forget names. He wanted his son to have a memorable one.

When Orlando was four years old, Harry Bloom died. To help raise Orlando and Samantha, Colin Stone stepped in. He became the children's guardian and helped support Sonia.

Both Bloom children loved to play dress-up. At age four, Orlando made his acting debut at the annual Kent

Festival. Dressed like an ape, he jumped around onstage. The costume was hot and sticky. Without thinking, Bloom reached behind him and scratched his butt. The audience went wild with laughter. Years later, he would still remember the embarrassment of that moment.

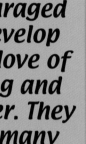

Samantha and her brother were encouraged to develop their love of acting and theater. They won many trophies and awards.

Samantha and her brother were encouraged to develop their love of acting and theater. They won many trophies and awards for their poetry and Bible readings. Sonia also took them to see plays and movies. The superheroes on television made an impression as well. "I just thought they were so awesome, and when I realized that I could be any of those characters, that was kind of what inspired me to sort of try and become an actor," says Bloom.

Orlando's young life truly was full of bumps and bruises. When he was one, his mother, who was carrying him, leaned over to pick something up and hit his head on a tree. It was his first skull fracture. A few months later, he fell off a kitchen stool and fractured it again. At age 11, he broke his leg skiing. At 12, he broke his nose and finger playing rugby. At 13, he broke his wrist while snowboarding.

While Bloom was great on stage and could tackle most outdoor activities, he struggled in school. He spent a lot of class time daydreaming about being outside. His mother was worried. She enrolled him in nearby St. Edmund's, an expensive private school. She also got him a job at the local

A young Bloom is already showing off the confidence and good looks that would one day command the attention of many fans.

shooting range as a clay trapper. He ran the machine that shot out bright orange clay disks. People would shoot at these flying disks to practice their aim.

Another reason Bloom had trouble in school was because he has a learning disability called dyslexia (dis-LEK-see-ah). Dyslexia makes it difficult for a person to read and understand what he or she is reading. Sonia worked closely with her son to help him with his schoolwork. Soon his grades were improving. It was just in time too. There were some big changes just around the corner.

A Different Kind
of Education

*B*loom's teenage years were exciting ones. When he was 13, his mother sat him down and gently explained that Harry Bloom was not really his father. Instead, his real father was Colin Stone, the man who had been helping the family for years. Although it was a shock, Bloom had come to love Stone. He could barely remember Harry. He grew to accept the idea. Today, he considers himself lucky to have had two loving fathers.

At 16, Bloom already knew that acting was what he wanted to do with his life. He also knew that he could not pursue that career in Kent. He decided to move to London. The National Youth Theatre had accepted him as one of their students.

For the first time, Bloom began to really enjoy school. He was learning not only about acting, but also about everything that went on behind the scenes. He had classes on stage management, lighting, sound, costuming, props, and scenery. "It was only when I went to drama school that I really started to appreciate education," he recalls.

Not all of his time was spent studying. Being young and far from his parents, Bloom had his wilder moments. He made friends with older students. Soon, he was spending nights dancing and drinking at clubs. To earn spending money, he worked in several trendy clothing stores. With his flare for fashion and his good looks, he fit in perfectly.

In 1994, Bloom got his first television role. He played a troubled teen on a British hospital drama called *Casualty*. Although it was a small part, he did it well.

The following year, Bloom was given a scholarship to the British American Drama Academy (BADA). It was quite an honor. Hundreds of students apply to this school and only a handful are chosen. Bloom studied at BADA for two years. He played countless roles there and learned important elements about acting.

Bloom studied at BADA for two years. He played countless roles there and learned important elements about acting.

In 1997, he moved on to Guildhall School of Music and Drama. During his time there, Bloom appeared in the movie *Wilde*, which was based on the life of writer Oscar Wilde. He had only one line, but it was enough to make an impression on both viewers and critics. He also appeared on a number of British television shows, including the popular crime series *Midsomer Murders*.

Acting offers began coming in, but Bloom turned most of them down. He wanted to finish his education first. At school, he was in a new show every other month. He was always memorizing the lines to something. Sometimes he would have the lead role; other times, a minor one.

> *Acting offers began coming in, but Bloom turned most of them down. He wanted to finish his education first.*

In his second year at Guildhall, Bloom had his near-fatal fall from the roof. Although he missed a few weeks of school, it was not long before he was back on the stage.

In 1999, with graduation just weeks away, big news arrived at Guildhall. Everyone was talking about the auditions being held for the upcoming *Lord of the Rings* movies. Students were sending in tapes of themselves, desperately hoping to get a part. Bloom decided to send in one as well. He hoped to get the part of the human Faramir.

To his surprise, Bloom was called in to read personally for Peter Jackson, the movie's director. Two days before he officially graduated, he got a call from Jackson. They had hired someone else to play Faramir, but how would he like the part of Legolas Greenleaf?

"I got this incredible phone call saying they were offering me the role," says Bloom. "It was like winning the lottery. Like having all your dreams fulfilled. It was amazing!"

Bloom was thrilled. His career was about to skyrocket in ways he could never have imagined.

The Lord of the Rings *trilogy was filmed in New Zealand, and Bloom became a huge fan of the island country's people and scenery.*

The World Meets "Legolas"

When Bloom agreed to join the cast of *The Lord of the Rings*, he had little idea what he was in for. *The Lord of the Rings* is a trilogy: It consists of three movies (*The Fellowship of the Ring*, *The Two Towers*, and *Return of the King*) based on the novels by J.R.R. Tolkien. Because Jackson planned to make all three movies in a row, it would take a year and a half to complete the filming — and that would be accomplished in New Zealand. It would be hard work, but Bloom would also learn new skills and make new friends.

The part of Legolas was difficult and demanding. It required not only wearing pointy ears, blue contact lenses, and a long blond wig, but also learning a whole new language and way of moving. Legolas was an Elf. In the world of the movie, these creatures are quiet, graceful, and immortal. They have excellent hearing and eyesight. In Legolas's case, they also have great aim.

To play the part, Bloom shaved his head down to a mohawk. That way dark hair would not show through any of the three $5,000 wigs he'd have to wear. For each day of shooting, he would spend two hours in makeup having the pointy ears put on. He'd spend another hour having them taken off.

Bloom learned how to move through the forest as if he were a part of it. "Legolas' moves are smooth and elegant, like a cat . . . it's very balletic," says Bloom. "It's also [very] hard to do without falling over!"

The transformation of the dark, curly haired Bloom to the blond Elf Legolas was amazing.

He was taught how to wield a sword with ease and shoot an arrow correctly. Within a week, he was able to shoot paper plates out of the sky. It took him longer to learn how to grab an arrow from behind him and not get it caught in his wig.

Finally, Bloom had to learn how to speak Elvish, a complete language author J.R.R. Tolkien had created for his books. A special teacher was brought in to teach him and fellow actors how to speak their lines in this language clearly and easily.

During the long filming process, the actors were told not to participate in any kind of dangerous sport. Bloom chose not to listen. The daredevil in him would not allow it. While he was in New Zealand, he went bungee jumping for the first time. He loved it so much, he did it six times in a row. He also learned how to surf, skydive, and go whitewater rafting. Despite his history, he did not get hurt. In fact, the only injury he suffered during the 18 months of filming was received on the set. He fell off his horse and hit a rock, breaking one of his ribs.

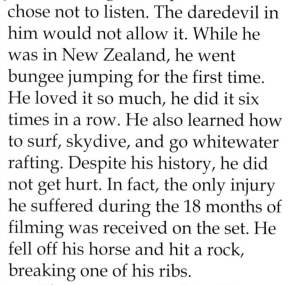

While he was in New Zealand, he went bungee jumping for the first time. He loved it so much, he did it six times in a row.

The pace was grueling. The actors worked 14 hours a day, six days a week. In the process, they all became very close friends. When shooting was finished, nine of them decided to get matching tattoos. Together, Sean Astin (Sam Gamgee), Dominic Monaghan (Merry), Billy Boyd (Pippin), Ian McKellen (Gandalf), Elijah Wood (Frodo Baggins), Sean Bean (Boromir), Viggo Mortenson (Aragorn), Brett Beattie (Gimli's stunt double), and Bloom had tattoos of the Elven word for nine put on various parts of their bodies. Bloom had his put on his forearm, since he was an archer in the movie.

When the first of the three *Lord of the Rings* movies came out, it was a complete and total success. Critics and audiences both were amazed by it. *The Fellowship of the Ring* was incredibly popular, and so were all of its stars. It was the Elf Legolas, however, who grabbed the most attention. Bloom's good looks and great acting impressed everyone. It was not long before posters and action figures of the characters were on the shelves. Wherever he went, Bloom was greeted by screaming fans and blinding camera flashes. He was shocked by the attention the movie brought him. He had never experienced anything like it.

He had a wonderful time making the trilogy. "I got to dress up in funny clothes and run around New Zealand with a bow and arrow for 18 months, how bad could that be?" he says.

Now that his time shooting arrows was over, it was time for a new adventure. This one would take him straight from fantasy to reality.

> *Wherever he went, Bloom was greeted by screaming fans and blinding camera flashes. He was shocked by the attention.*

A Soldier and a Pirate

*B*loom had all the movie offers he could want. He moved to Los Angeles and started on his next project, a serious movie based on history.

In 1993, eighteen U.S. soldiers were killed and more than 70 others were wounded in the country of Somalia in eastern Africa. During the battle, Private First Class Todd Blackburn fell out of a helicopter and broke his back. The movie *Black Hawk Down* tells about how the other soldiers stayed with him until he was rescued. Their motto was "Leave no man behind."

To prepare for the role, the actors spent time in boot camp finding out what it was like to be a soldier. They learned how to tie knots, use military radios, and fire M16A2 rifles.

Unlike the role of Legolas, the part of Blackburn did not make many physical demands on Bloom. Most of his onscreen time was spent lying on the ground in pain. Just thinking back to his own fall helped him prepare for that.

The only new thing he had to learn was an American accent.

Black Hawk Down was released in 2001. It was not a blockbuster like The Fellowship of the Ring, but that was not surprising. They were two totally different kinds of movies and appealed to different audiences.

The Two Towers came out in 2002, and once again, Orlandomania hit the United States. Young girls across the country had posters of Bloom on their bedroom walls. His face was on every teen magazine. Fans became known as Bloomatics. He typically received over 500 fan letters every week. He began winning a string of awards, including Best Breakthrough Male at the MTV Movie Awards; Britain's Empire Award for Best Debut; Best Newcomer from SFX magazine's Top 10 Sexiest Men; Teen People's 25 Hottest Stars under 25; AOL Moviegoers Award for Best Supporting Actor; and Best Actor of 2003 from Rolling Stone magazine.

The Two Towers came out in 2002, and once again, Orlandomania hit the United States.

It came as a surprise then when he decided to star in a modest little Australian movie called Ned Kelly about some Irish outlaws. Once again, it was based on real people and events. This time, for his part as Joseph Byrne, Bloom had to learn an Irish accent. Soon after Ned Kelly hit theaters, the third installment of the Lord of the Rings movies, Return of the King, was released. It was just as popular as the first two.

Bloom appreciates all the awards he has been given. In 2002, he received the Empire Award for Best Debut in London.

It was Bloom's next part, however, that catapulted him to movie stardom. This time he played Will Turner in *Pirates of the Caribbean: The Curse of the Black Pearl*. For this role, he had to learn how to fence. It took hours and hours of practice. Although he had handled a sword as Legolas, this sport was much more challenging. "It was a lot harder," he recalls. "There are a lot more moves. There's a lot to learn. That was a huge sequence, particularly that opening scene. I was quite intimidated by the whole idea of having to do that."

One of his costars was Johnny Depp, an actor Bloom had admired for years. The two of them blended perfectly, and the movie was a smash hit. It was so popular that two sequels were made. *Pirates of the Caribbean: Dead Man's Chest* was released in July 2006. The other was scheduled for release in 2007.

Bloom knows he has had a wonderful life and career so far. As he put it, "I've been an elf, a soldier boy, . . . a pirate, and an outlaw. I really am every living boy's dream."

> *Johnny Depp and Bloom blended perfectly, and the movie was a smash hit.*

Bloom's role as the fencing, romantic lead in Pirates of the Caribbean *shot him right to stardom.*

A Bright Future

The years 2004 and 2005 were extremely busy for Bloom. In 2004, he starred in a small film called *The Calcium Kid*. For the very first time, he had the leading role. He played a milkman who, by a strange twist of fate, got the chance to fight in the ring with a boxing champion. For that role, Bloom had to learn basic boxing moves. He also had to gain weight and build up his muscles. This comedy, however, was not a big hit. Bloom did not like how it felt to produce something less than successful.

Fortunately, the feeling did not last long. His next role was playing Prince Paris in the Greek drama *Troy*. In it, he was the handsome man who stole Helen's heart and in doing so started a terrible ten-year war. *Troy* also starred Brad Pitt and Eric Bana. Next, it was the role of Balian in *Kingdom of Heaven*. The focus in this movie was the Christian Crusades in 12th-century Jerusalem. Both movies required Bloom to play very dramatic and intense roles.

They also highlighted the good looks that he had become known for.

In 2005, Bloom also starred in *Elizabethtown* with Kirsten Dunst. In this film, he plays Drew Baylor, a man dealing with the sudden death of his father. During the filming, Bloom was rumored to be dating his costar. There was nothing new about that. Every time he starred in a film, the media reported suspected romances. One week it was a model. The next it was an actress. Although he has dated many different women, Bloom has had an on-and-off relationship with actress Kate Bosworth for several years.

> By age 29, Bloom had already achieved more stardom than many other actors. His face was known all over the world.

There is little doubt that Bloom's future is bright. Besides the sequels to *Pirates of the Caribbean*, he also played a character named Hollywood Paolo in *Love and Other Disasters*.

By age 29, Bloom had already achieved more stardom than many other actors. His face was known all over the world. When he auctioned a handprint on a T-shirt for the BBC charity Children In Need, money rolled in. When his mother decided to take the stamps from his endless fan letters and donate them to the Strode Park Foundation for Disabled People in Herne, England, he was happy to oblige. The foundation specializes in helping people with back problems, and Bloom certainly remembers needing that kind of help.

Bloom and Elizabethtown *costar Kirsten Dunst were rumored to be sweethearts, but they are actually just good friends.*

Whether audiences come to see him because of his looks, his acting ability, or a combination of the two, the bottom line is that they will keep coming. He is a true star of the new millennium.

Now and then, Bloom reflects on his traumatic and frightening fall of years ago. He still feels pain from it but sees a purpose for it. "Having a little bit of pain with my back reminds me of just how lucky I am," he says. "It also focuses me and refocuses me to make everything a bit more real."

CHRONOLOGY

1977	Born Orlando Jonathan Blanchard Bloom in Kent, England, on January 13, to Harry and Sonia Bloom
1981	Harry Bloom dies
1990	Finds out his real father is Colin Stone
1993	Moves to London to attend the National Youth Theatre
1994	Appears on British television in *Casualty*
1995	Attends the British American Drama Academy on a scholarship
1997	Enrolls at Guildhall School of Music and Drama; lands first movie role
1998	Falls from a roof terrace
1999	Graduates from Guildhall; begins filming *The Lord of the Rings* movies
2001	Moves to Los Angeles, California
2002	Wins multiple awards
2003	Begins relationship with actress Kate Bosworth
2005	Breaks up and reunites with Kate Bosworth
2006	Films *Pirates of the Caribbean: Dead Man's Chest* and the third *Pirates of the Caribbean* movie in the trilogy

2002	Empire Award for Best Debut; MTV Movie Award for Breakthrough Male Performance
2003	NBR Award for Best Ensemble Performance; Hollywood Discovery Award for Breakthrough Acting—Male
2004	BFCA Award for Best Acting Ensemble; Screen Actors Guild Award for Outstanding Performance by a Cast in a Motion Picture

FILMOGRAPHY

1994	*Wilde*
2001	*The Lord of the Rings: Fellowship of the Ring*
2002	*Black Hawk Down*
	The Lord of the Rings: The Two Towers
2003	*Pirates of the Caribbean: The Curse of the Black Pearl*
	Ned Kelly
	The Lord of the Rings: The Return of the King
2004	*The Calcium Kid*
	Troy
	Haven
2005	*Kingdom of Heaven*
	Elizabethtown
2006	*Love and Other Disasters*
	Pirates of the Caribbean: Dead Man's Chest

Books

Boer, Peter. *Orlando Bloom: Shooting to Stardom*. Edmonton, Canada: Icon Press, 2005.

Kranenburg, Heather. *Lovin' Bloom: The Unauthorized Story of Orlando Bloom*. New York: Ballantine Books, 2004.

Parfitt, A.C. *Orlando Bloom: The Biography; The Amazing True Story of Britain's Hottest New Star*. London, England: John Blake Publishing, 2004.

Steele, Robert. *Orlando Bloom*. London, England: Plexus Publishing, 2004.

Works Consulted

Abrahamian, Line. "The Kid Stays in the Picture." *Reader's Digest UK*, August 2005.

Barker, Lynn. "One on One with Orlando." August 29, 2005. Teen Hollywood.com http://www.teenhollywood.com/d.asp?r=105558&c=1038

Hatty, Michele. "It's His Time to Bloom." *USA Weekend*, April 29–May 1, 2005.

Murray, Rebecca. "Orlando Bloom Takes on a Different Type of Character in *Elizabethtown*. October 9, 2005. http://movies.about.com/od/elizabethtown/a/elizabob100905.htm

Otto, Jeff. "An Interview with Orlando Bloom and Liv Tyler." December 17, 2003. http://filmforce.ign.com/articles/446/446476p1.html

Roston, Tom. "Orlando Bloom: Summer All-Star." *Premiere*. http://www.premiere.com/article.asp?section_id= 6&article_id=1014

Strauss, Neil. "Chasing Orlando." *Rolling Stone*, May 19, 2003.

"Ultimate Tribute to Orlando Bloom," *Life Story* magazine, 2005.

On the Internet
Full Bloom
http://www.full-bloom.net/
The One Ring: "Orlando Bloom"
http://www.theonering.net/movie/cast/bloom.html
Orlando Bloom Central
http://www.orlandocentral.net/
OrlandoBloomFans.com
http://orlandobloomfans.com/
The Orlando Bloom Files
http://www.theorlandobloomfiles.com/